Disney MOVIE MAGIC

A piano accompaniment book (HL00841177) is available for this collection.

D1313909

Disney characters and artwork © Disney Enterprises, Inc.

ISBN 0-7935-7836-1

HAL•LEONARD® CORPORATION

7777 W. BLUEMOUND RD. P.O. BOX 13819 MILWAUKEE, WI 53213

For all works contained herein:
Unauthorized copying, arranging, adapting, recording or public performance is an infringement of copyright.
Infringers are liable under the law.

Visit Hal Leonard Online at
www.halleonard.com

OUT OF THIN AIR

from Walt Disney's ALADDIN AND THE KING OF THIEVES

Alto Sax

Words and Music by
DAVID FRIEDMAN

© 1996 Walt Disney Music Company
International Copyright Secured   All Rights Reserved

CAN YOU FEEL THE LOVE TONIGHT
from Walt Disney Pictures' THE LION KING

Alto Sax

Music by ELTON JOHN
Lyrics by TIM RICE

© 1994 Wonderland Music Company, Inc.
International Copyright Secured   All Rights Reserved

CIRCLE OF LIFE

from Walt Disney Pictures' THE LION KING

Alto Sax

Music by ELTON JOHN
Lyrics by TIM RICE

© 1994 Wonderland Music Company, Inc.
International Copyright Secured   All Rights Reserved

HAKUNA MATATA
from Walt Disney Pictures' THE LION KING

Alto Sax

Music by ELTON JOHN
Lyrics by TIM RICE

© 1994 Wonderland Music Company, Inc.
International Copyright Secured   All Rights Reserved

I JUST CAN'T WAIT TO BE KING

from Walt Disney Pictures' THE LION KING

Alto Sax

Music by ELTON JOHN
Lyrics by TIM RICE

© 1994 Wonderland Music Company, Inc.
International Copyright Secured   All Rights Reserved

THIS LAND
from Walt Disney Pictures' THE LION KING

Alto Sax

Music by
HANS ZIMMER

© 1994 Wonderland Music Company, Inc.
International Copyright Secured   All Rights Reserved

THE VIRGINIA COMPANY

from Walt Disney's POCAHONTAS

Alto Sax

Music by ALAN MENKEN
Lyrics by STEPHEN SCHWARTZ

© 1995 Wonderland Music Company, Inc. and Walt Disney Music Company
International Copyright Secured   All Rights Reserved

COLORS OF THE WIND

from Walt Disney's POCAHONTAS

Alto Sax

Music by ALAN MENKEN
Lyrics by STEPHEN SCHWARTZ

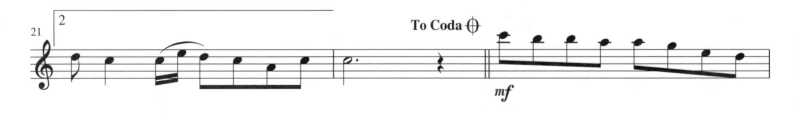

© 1995 Wonderland Music Company, Inc. and Walt Disney Music Company
International Copyright Secured   All Rights Reserved

JUST AROUND THE RIVERBEND

from Walt Disney's POCAHONTAS

Alto Sax

Music by ALAN MENKEN
Lyrics by STEPHEN SCHWARTZ

© 1995 Wonderland Music Company, Inc. and Walt Disney Music Company
International Copyright Secured   All Rights Reserved

MINE, MINE, MINE
from Walt Disney's POCAHONTAS

Alto Sax

Music by ALAN MENKEN
Lyrics by STEPHEN SCHWARTZ

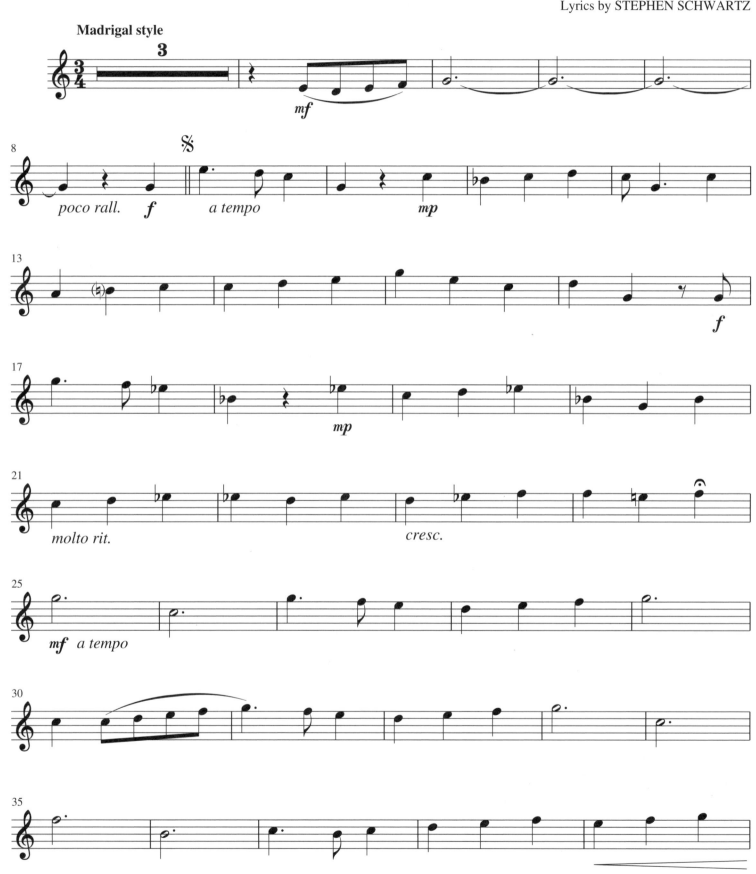

© 1995 Wonderland Music Company, Inc. and Walt Disney Music Company
International Copyright Secured   All Rights Reserved

CRUELLA DE VIL
from Walt Disney's 101 DALMATIANS

Alto Sax

Words and Music by
MEL LEVEN

© 1959 Walt Disney Music Company
Copyright Renewed
International Copyright Secured   All Rights Reserved

(higher notes optional)

FORGET ABOUT LOVE
from Walt Disney's THE RETURN OF JAFAR

Alto Sax

Words and Music by
MICHAEL SILVERSHER and PATTY SILVERSHER

© 1994 Wonderland Music Company, Inc.
International Copyright Secured   All Rights Reserved

YOU'VE GOT A FRIEND IN ME

from Walt Disney's TOY STORY

Alto Sax

Music and Lyrics by
RANDY NEWMAN

© 1995 Walt Disney Music Company
International Copyright Secured   All Rights Reserved

STRANGE THINGS

from Walt Disney's TOY STORY

Alto Sax

Music and Lyrics by
RANDY NEWMAN

© 1995 Walt Disney Music Company
International Copyright Secured   All Rights Reserved